MIRYAM OF NAZARETH

Woman of Strength & Wisdom

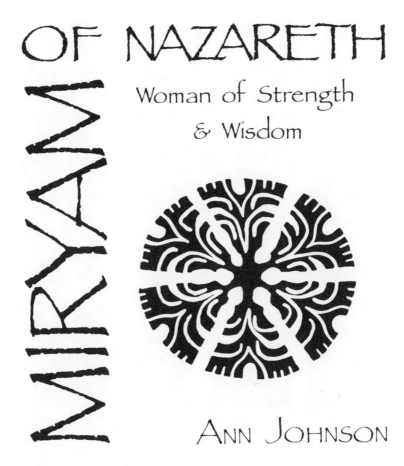

ANN JOHNSON

MIRYAM OF NAZARETH

Woman of Strength
& Wisdom

ANN JOHNSON

Ave Maria Press • Notre Dame, Indiana 46556

About the Author:

Ann Johnson is a resident of Weston, Vermont, where she is a self-employed consultant for education and parenting. She is a mother of five children and received her education at Northwestern University and Antioch College. She has participated in the International Marian Research Institute at the University of Dayton, and notes that "it is a personal source of joy to uncover the treasure existing in the life and witness of Mary for my own life and perhaps, I hope, for the lives of others."

First printing, August, 1984
Fourth printing, July, 1986
52,500 copies in print

Acknowledgments:

Excerpts from *The Jerusalem Bible*, copyright © 1966 by Darton, Longman & Todd, Ltd. and Doubleday & Company, Inc. Used with permission of the publisher.

The following editions were also used for reference: The *New American Bible*, the *Authorized Version of King James*, and the *Nestle Greek Text With Literal Translation* by Rev. Alfred Marshall, D. Litt.

Library of Congress Catalog Card Number: 84-71347

International Standard Book Number: 0-87793-320-0 (Cloth)
0-87793-321-9 (Paper)

Cover design: Thomas Ringenberg

Printed and bound in the United States of America.

for Melanie Ann Spaulding
and her family

CONTENTS

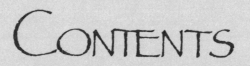

INTRODUCTION

Miryam of Nazareth is the story of one particular woman's life in living dialogue with Yahweh, the One God, the One Who Is. This book was written to re-present a strong, appropriate and theologically stimulating vision of living faith as expressed by a woman of the Bible. I have used free verse grounded in traditional biblical poetry to tell this story.

The woman of the story is the person who was the one witness of the entire drama of Jesus' life, the woman we now call the Greek name Mary, a woman deeply rooted in her religious Jewish history. According to the *American Heritage* dictionary the root of the name Mary is the Hebrew *Miryam* meaning "rebellion." How fitting for a people called to be a people of God, often in conflict with political authorities, whose infant sons were at times systematically slain by alien rulers, to name their daughters "hope of change." And indeed, the daughters of Zion have a rich heroic tradition. According to Hebrew history Jewish heroines were active seekers of salvation and rescue for Israel. They were strong and powerful, strikingly assertive individuals. From Genesis to Acts there is a line of women living lives of religious vitality, cultural integrity and political involvement while performing deeds which powerfully transformed the nation of Israel and ultimately the modern world.

Whether in the role of prophet, judge, warrior, matriarch, lover or liturgical psalmist the women of the covenant shared a common pattern of relationship with their God. Grounded in deep prayer, liturgical observance, celebration and communal sensitivity these women moved out to speak and act in ways which turned around the Hebrew community both historically and perceptually. In the true fashion of rebels, they made war on faithlessness, hopelessness, and narrow-mindedness. They questioned, searched, changed and led their families and their nations into new understandings of relationship with God and with one another.

Many modern women have found it useful to unearth ancient female goddess figures for models of a feminine one who reaches into the life and spirit of earth and heaven. Others have turned away in anger from a Mary ill-used to contort their own individuality by fearful though well-meaning parents, priests and teachers. I, too, am a modern woman intent on searching out the "feminine face of God" and I find that the gospel traditions are rich in energy and wisdom for the needs of our time. If Mary is type of the church, then she is witness, she is prayer and she is disciple. She is celebrant. If she is model of Christians then she is a faithful Jewish woman who reached into mystery and courageously drew herself anew. If she is Mother of God then she is somehow foundation, companion and potential. If she is Mother of God then she is a point of unity within which all people of all faiths may search for commonality.

This book is constructed in three sections recapitulating Miryam's life possibilities 1) in the captive Israel of the longing and faithful people, 2) in Jerusalem of the living Jesus and the summoning community and 3) in the Israel of the resurrection community. The theme of each period of her life is grounded in prayer and action springing from the consequences of her human growth and faith experiences: First in the nourishing and enabling traditions of her heritage as detailed in the Hebrew Bible, then in the life-changing experiences with Jesus and her immediate situation retold in the Christian Bible, and finally centered in the people, spirit and house churches of the Acts community.

The central form of the book is a collection of Magnificats. This form of praise and petition is grounded in Hebrew biblical tradition and would have been well-known to her. The Magnificat prayer form is a concise and powerful expression of the totality of the God-human relationship, that dialogue which turns the world inside out, confirms our history and calls us to remember and renew. This poem form expresses the rich and extremely effective feminine approach to a life lived in consort with a creative God. Mary as a woman made in the eternal image and reflecting that image is a woman who lives and expresses her God relationship in its fullest potential.

Our most familiar theology has traditionally called us to a spirituality which transcends our humanity. I envision this woman issuing a companion call to a humanity which transcends our spirituality. A humanity so simply lived that we do not "practice" spiritual rigors to condition ourselves for closeness to God. A humanity so filled with the love of God/neighbor that the Word is commonly spoken in simple miracles of God-bearing, healing, sharing, transfiguring and Shalom. Spoken in song and dance, in loving rememberings of those who have gone before and in rejoicing embraces of those we talk with, feed, nurture and with whom we celebrate.

A Beginning

My God
Adonai
For what is Israel's story of our life with you,
    if not for now?
Figure of my people,
    Why do you exist if not to be for us in this moment?
In the tremor of our song we have carried you from age to age,
    song lifting hope into the tremor of these times.
Guiding fire
Clarifying light
    For whom the story told if not for me;
    for whom the storyteller if not for you, Yahweh?
Yahweh, One Who Is, becoming
    the story drawn from storehouses of a people's legend
    scratched in stone and skin, branded in communal memory,
    store on store of lingering images born in the
    Ark of Throbbing Promises
    whispered in the hollow cave of desert blown linen
    rustling in the Holy Wind.

My God
Adonai
One who leads us through the desert
One who leads us through the raging sea
As the kinswomen of my heritage walked
        shoulder to shoulder
        stride for stride
You looked upon us who were Israel and you walked with us.

My God
Adonai
Like my kinsman Moses, I come to the mountain of God.
You who will be what you will be,
        restore and reconsecrate my heart and mind,
        the hearts and minds of all the called of God.
One that is
One who hears
One who becomes aware
One who leads us into freedom
Whom have you chosen for a people?
If not us, who?

You who are ancient of days,
      before all morning and night,
come to those who live Torah.
Have you not promised you would come?
If not now, when?
God of our history
God of our days
We stand again at the foot of your mountain.
We stand as it seems in the last days.
If there is to be a tomorrow, speak again.
Bestow again Torah.

MAGNIFICAT
OF
BETROTHAL

Our souls are filled with wonder at the gift of our loving,
    and our spirits take on new meaning in the giving of love,
    God of the Flowing Well,
    you have looked upon us with favor as we join our lives
    in response to you.
Yes, from this time on all people who look upon us
    will recognize us as being life companions
    and will call us blessed,
    for you, the One who dwells in human hearts,
    have done great things for us.
Holy, is your name,
    and your confirming joy reaches from age to age
    to those who dare to journey
    on the unknown pathways of committed love.
You have shown us the life-changing power of our love
    in the eyes of those who know us and
    in the richness of our work.
You have humbled us by the intensity of our otherness.
The false pride that we treasured in our ability to stand alone,
    has been cast aside
    and we understand ourselves and you more tenderly
    as we begin to experience the treasure
    of a lifetime of standing together.

We are no longer lonely:
> We touch with compassion those who come to us filled with
> needs.

You have opened the doors of eternity to us
> as we searched for you,
> mindful of your own longings for a people to love
> . . . according to the dreams and murmurings you have shared
> with those who love since the beginning of time . . .
> mindful of your own longings for a people to love,
> we recognize that the bondedness of human hearts and lives
> reflects one true reality of you, the Living God.

THE PRAYER OF MIRYAM IN THE DESERT

In the days when Judea was oppressed in the reign of King Herod,
    there lived a woman named Miryam.

Miryam who listened:
    listened to the songs in the Temple
    listened to the stories of her people
    listened to the talk in the market
    listened to the fear in the streets
    listened to the prayers at her table
    listened to the stirrings in her heart.

Miryam who wondered:
    wondered at the look of passive faces
    wondered at the glare of angry eyes
    wondered at the failure of the Maccabees
    wondered at the Law so joylessly fulfilled
    wondered at the hopes of her community
    wondered at the passions in her soul.

Miryam who knew:
    knew the promises of Yahweh
    knew the heritage of Israel from Abraham and Sarah
    knew the lifelessness in captive people
    knew the mercy of the Lord on those who seek justice
    knew the fervent hopes of those she loved
    knew the possibility within a life held open to the touch of God.

The hope of Israel's resurrection rose in Miryam's heart.
The seed of rebels, echoed in her name, sprung life-bound from her
        spirit.
The tradition of her people called forth in her an energy tough-bounded
        by her vision.
Ash covered and sack clothed
    she walked into the desert.
Miryam entered God's wilderness in longing
     to bring her people home.

My God
Yahweh
To what mountain have you fled?
Within what cavern have you hid?
I am your people.
I am Israel and
I call to you.

Daily I listen for evidence of your vitality.
I hear only shallow resonances of what once was.

Daily I hear stories of our past with you.
Exodus and prophecy seem old and far away.

Daily I witness a beaten people begging alms and hanging on a Ro-
       man tree.
Your law rots, twisted and suppressed in Roman hands.

My God
Yahweh
Have you forgotten who we are?
Are we forsaken by a love grown cold and faithless?
I am named Miryam.
I am Hebrew and
I claim my hour with you.

I remind you of the covenant forever binding on us both.
I call on you to honor it.

I sound forth Isaiah's promise . . . Prince of Peace, Redeemer, King.
I do not come in knowledge, but in hope.

I implore you in this hour to fulfill our destiny.
I stand with Deborah and with Ruth willing to risk everything.

My God
Yahweh
Crushed spirits cry, "Messiah."
Compromised, defeated, "Now, Messiah."
Born in the bloodline of the desert priests,
     betrothed to David's house,
What place I have I do not know, but
I am here.

REFLECTIONS ON DEBORAH

Yahweh, my God.
It is I, Miryam.
You are the Savior of my people.
In you I trust.
Age after age we have come to you in the hour of our distress.
Never have you failed us.
You have been steadfast.
You are our God, One Alone.
And we are a people, fully yours.

In the days of your prophet Deborah
You saved Israel by the hand of a woman.
In quiet wisdom she stood beneath her tree.
    guiding the searching ones in your Law.
She saw the threat of tyranny to her simple people.
She came to you for help and you answered her.
She listened.

Deborah went out from her walk with you and called the commander of
       Israel, Barak, and she instructed him according to what you had
       told her.
He was afraid.
And so Deborah stood up and went with Barak to Kedesh.
Yes, ten thousand men marched behind him and Deborah marched
       with him.
Leading Barak with his ten thousand she went up to Mount Tabor.
Together they watched the mighty chariots of Sisera gather.
Together they stormed the milling armies,
Calling your name.
Leading Israel into the unknown.
And you, Yahweh, struck terror into the hearts of Sisera's army and
       they fled.
From the hand of the woman Jael,
    Deborah received the life of Sisera.
In the temple we hear her song:

"That warriors in Israel unbound their hair,
that the people came forward with a will,
for this, bless Yahweh!

"Listen, you kings! Give ear, you princes!
From me, from me comes a song for Yahweh.
I will glorify Yahweh, God of Israel.

"Dead, dead were Israel's villages
until you rose up, O Deborah,
you rose up, a mother in Israel.

"Awake, awake, Deborah!
Awake, awake, declaim a song!

"Blessed be Jael among women . . .
among all women that dwell in tents may she be blessed.

"So perish all your enemies, Yahweh!
And let those who love you be like the sun
when he arises in all his strength!"

Savior of my People, One Alone
As Deborah trusted you,
     so do I trust.
As Deborah saw her people threatened,
     so do I see my people threatened.
As Deborah prayed to you for help,
     so do I pray for help.
As Deborah listened and went out,
     so would I listen.
As Deborah offered her all in your service,
     so do I offer my all.
As Deborah knew Israel to be saved by the hand of a woman,
     so do I know this possibility.
As Deborah rose up a mother in Israel,
     so would I rise
     I, Miryam, a mother for my people.
Hear me, my God
and have mercy on me.

Reflections on Judith

In the days of the faithful widow Judith
You saved Israel by the hand of a woman.
In prayer and fasting she lived in solitude with you.
Then came the might of Nebuchadnezzar
    when all the world lay prone before him.
He sent his captain Holofernes to claim Israel's land.
Joakim, high priest, commanded Israel to resist . . .
    "Occupy the mountain passes and prepare for war."
As Holofernes roared in angry rage at the resistance of this moun-
    tain people
All Jerusalem, ash covered, fell beseeching at your feet.
Sack clothed they cried to you
and you looked kindly on them.

The cavalry of Holofernes advanced and seized the water points that
    quenched the thirst of Israel.
Bitter cries rose up from the parched throats of your faithful and
    Uzziah set a limit on your mercy.
Judith left her widow's rooms and chastised Uzziah.
    "You dare not test Yahweh.
    Let us take up the challenge and give thanks for the testing.
    As God does this moment search our hearts
    So will we rise to the ordeal held out by Yahweh to Israel.
    Israel who lives so near to Yahweh's heart.
    Before the time fixed by you for surrendering the town
    God will make use of me to rescue Israel."

Having said this much Judith came to you, O God
    In sackcloth and tears she came.
Ash-covered words blew in the desert dust.

    "God, my God,
    now hear this widow too;
    for you have made the past,
    and what is happening now, and what will follow.
    What is, what will be, you have planned;
    what has been, you designed.

    "See, the Assyrians, boasting in their army.
    Trust as they may in shield and spear,
    in bow and sling,
    in you they have not recognized
    the Lord, the shatterer of war;
    yours alone the title of Lord.

"For they plan to profane your holy places,
to defile the tabernacle, the resting place of your glorious name.
Observe their arrogance,
send your fury on their heads,
give the needful courage
to this widow's hand.
Break their pride
by a woman's hand.

"Your strength does not lie in numbers,
nor your might in violent men;
since you are the God of the humble,
the help of the oppressed,
the support of the weak,
the refuge of the forsaken,
the savior of the despairing.

"Please, please, God of my father,
God of the heritage of Israel,
Master of heaven and earth,
Creator of the waters,
King of your whole creation,
hear my prayer.
And demonstrate to every nation, every tribe,
that you are Yahweh, God almighty, all-powerful,
and that the race of Israel
has you for sole protector."

Her prayer finished, Judith washed.
She arrayed herself most beautifully and
the people of Bethulia gasped in awe and admiration
so exquisite her beauty, so strong and calm her face.
Led by Uzziah, village voices swelled in benediction,
  "May the God of our ancestors keep you in his favor!
  May he grant your purposes fulfilment
  to the glory of the sons of Israel,
  to the greater glory of Jerusalem!"

Chosen and composed Judith and her maid went out
  from the gates of her town and
  into the camp of Holofernes
  into the midst of the enemy camp.
Her beauty mellowed the Assyrian hearts.
Her facile words portrayed the situation as other than it was.
Her devoutness quieted their caution.
And so events proceeded which drew Holofernes
  to death at Judith's hand and all Assyria's army
  fled wildly in their terror
  ripped at their tunics as they ran.

In darkest night,
With gory evidence Judith climbed the hill to Bethulia
Shouting to the guards as she approached the gates:
  "Open the gate! Open!
  For the Lord our God is with us still,
    displaying his strength in Israel."
By firelight the people crowded round.
Her declamation validated by the contents of the bloody bag.
Falling on their knees the people worshiped God.
Then Uzziah said to Judith:
  "May you be blessed, my daughter, by God Most High,
    beyond all women on earth;
  and may the Lord God be blessed,
    the Creator of heaven and earth,
    by whose guidance you cut off the head
    of the leader of our enemies.
  The trust you have shown
    shall not pass from the memories of men,
    but shall ever remind them
    of the power of God.
  God grant you to be always held in honor,
    and rewarded with blessings,
    since you did not consider your own life
    when our nation was brought to its knees,
    but warded off our ruin,
    walking undeterred before God."
All the people answered, "Amen! Amen!"

Joakim the high priest and the Council of High Priests came from
      Jerusalem, came to see Judith and they blessed her saying:

   "You are the glory of Jerusalem!
   You are the great pride of Israel!
   You are the highest honor of our race!

   "By doing all this with your own hand
   you have deserved well of Israel,
   and God has approved what you have done.

   "May you be blessed by the Lord Almighty
   in all the days to come!"

All the people answered, "Amen! Amen!"

All the people celebrated Judith.
The women of Israel, hurrying to see her,
      formed choirs of dancers in her honor.
Judith distributed branches to the women who accompanied her.
She and her companions put on wreaths of olive.
Then she took her place at the head of the procession
      and led the women as they danced.
All the men of Israel, armed and garlanded
      followed them singing hymns.
With all Israel around her,
Judith broke into this song of thanksgiving and
the whole people sang this hymn aloud.

"Praise my God with the tambourine,
Sing to the Lord with cymbal,
let psalm and canticle mingle for him,
extol his name, invoke it!
For the Lord is a God who shatters war,
he has pitched his camp in the middle of the people.

"Assyria came down from the mountains of the north,
came with tens of thousands of his army . . .
but the Lord Almighty has thwarted them
by a woman's hand.

"I will sing a new song to my God.
Lord, you are great, you are glorious,
wonderfully strong, unconquerable
May your whole creation serve you!
You spoke and things came into being,
you sent your breath and they were put together,
and no one can resist your voice.

"Should mountains topple
to mingle with the waves,
should rocks melt
like wax before your face,
to those who fear you
you would still be merciful.
Whoever walks with the Most High is great forever."

Savior of my People, One Alone
As Judith lived in faithfulness of prayer and fasting,
    so would I live.
As Judith heard the panic of a threatened people,
    so do I hear my people cry.
As Judith pled for wisdom in the testing,
    so I do pray for wisdom in the saving challenge.
As Judith went devoutly into the unknown,
    so would I go. Send me.
As Judith gave her hand to be the implement of rescue,
    so do I give my hand to you.
As Judith danced her joy in you,
    so will I dance.
I, Miryam, would dance and sing with my people in everlasting
    freedom before you, Yahweh in whom all things come into
    being.
Hear me, my God
and have mercy on me.

Reflections on Esther

In the days of the beautiful Esther
You saved Israel by the hand of a woman.
In graceful obedience the young Hadassah came before
  Ahasuerus, mighty king.
In regal dignity she remained within the court as Esther,
  admired queen.
In devoted silence she concealed her race and kindred
  as advised by Mordecai.
Mordecai, the dreamer,
  dreamed of a river and of dragons.
Mordecai, the faithful one,
  faithful to God and king.
Mordecai, who bowed only to Yahweh
  and so incurred the fateful wrath of Haman.
Thus the *pur* was cast revealing day and month of Haman's revenge.
A day proposed by Haman to the king for
  "destruction, slaughter and annihilation of all Jews,
  young and old, women and children,
  on the one day, the thirteenth day of the twelfth month,
  which is Adar,
  and the seizing of their possessions."
King Ahasuerus signed the edict and sealed it with his ring.
Thus the *pur* was cast.

Horror spread through Jewish homes.
A wailing loud and bitter from the mouth of Israel.
A people fell as one before you, Yahweh,
      garments torn, crying for your help.
Esther, queen, sent out inquiries from her isolated splendor.
What pain could rend such cries from the hearts of the
      people of her secret heart?
Mordecai responded with the plea for her to act.
      "Remember Esther, humbler days.
      Remember Esther, who you are.
         Invoke the Most High.
         Speak to King Ahasuerus for us and
         save us from death."
Esther replied,
      "I cannot speak unsummoned.
      Death is certain for one who speaks before the king unsummoned."
From Mordecai:
      "Esther, you are a Jew.
      Death awaits you either way.
      If you deny your choice to speak, relief will come from another
         place for us, but not for you and yours.
      Who knows? Perhaps you have come to the throne for just such a
         time as this."

Esther listened to Mordecai's prophetic challenge.
She knew herself to be stretched between two lives.
She was Esther, bride of power's throne and
She was Hadassah, woman of God's Covenant.
Resolve seized the heart of Esther and she chose!

Deepened and aware she spoke:
Her words were carried out by faithful messengers from the palace
        grounds.
    "Gather our people in prayer and fasting to support me.
    I will go before the king.
    And if I die, I die."

Three days they prayed.
Three days they fasted.
    "And all Israel cried out with all their might,
        for they were faced with death."

And Esther?
Esther feared.
Esther also took refuge with the Lord in the mortal peril which had over-
taken her. She took off her sumptuous robes and put on sorrowful
mourning. Instead of her expensive perfumes she covered her head with
ashes and dung. She humbled her body severely and the former scenes of
her happiness and elegance were now littered with tresses torn from her
hair. She besought the Lord God of Israel in these words:

"My Lord, our King, the only one,
come to my help, for I am alone
and have no helper but you
and am about to take my life in my hands.

"I have been taught from my earliest years, in the bosom of my
family, that you, Lord, chose
Israel out of all the nations
and our ancestors out of all the people of old times
to be your heritage for ever;
and that you have treated them as you promised.

"But then we sinned against you,
and you handed us over to our enemies
for paying honor to their gods.
Lord, you are just.

"But even now they are not satisfied
with the bitterness of our slavery:
they have put their hands in the hands of their idols
to abolish the decree that your own lips have uttered,
to blot out your heritage,
to stop the mouths of those who praise you,
to quench your altar and the glory of your House,
and instead to open the mouths of the heathen,
to sing the praise of worthless idols
and forever to idolize a king of flesh.

"Do not yield your scepter, Lord,
to non-existent beings.
Never let men mock at our ruin.
Turn their designs against themselves,
and make an example of him who leads the attack on us.
Remember, Lord; reveal yourself
in the time of our distress.

"As for me, give me courage,
King of gods and master of all power.
Put persuasive words into my mouth
when I face the lion;
change his feeling into hatred for our enemy,
that the latter and all like him may be brought to their end.

"As for ourselves, save us by your hand,
and come to my help, for I am alone
and have no one but you, Lord.
You have knowledge of all things,
and you know that I hate honors from the godless.
Nor has your handmaid found pleasure
from the day of her promotion until now
except in you, Lord, God of Abraham.
O God, whose strength prevails over all,
listen to the voice of the desperate,
save us from the hand of the wicked,
and free me from my fear."

On the third day, when she had finished praying, she took off her suppliant's mourning attire and dressed herself in her full splendor. Radiant as she then appeared, she invoked God who watches over all men and saves them. Then she took two maids with her. She leaned on the maid's arm as though languidly, but in fact because her body was too weak to support her. Rosy with the full flush of her beauty, her face radiated joy and love; but her heart shrank with fear. Having passed through door after door, she found herself in the presence of the king. He was seated on the royal throne—a formidable sight. But God changed the king's heart and he said to her . . . "What is the matter, Esther? I am your brother. Take heart; you will not die." Raising his golden scepter he laid it on her neck. "Speak to me."

And so began the weaving of events that brought the envious Haman to his death and gained for Israel by royal decree the right to come together to defend themselves.

Israel rose up in the month of Adar.
Israel rose up in strength.
In the cities and in the villages they fought for life.
In the cities and in the villages they took no plunder.
In the land the people rejoiced with feasting, with dancing,
    and by exchanging portions with each other.

Mordecai, the scribe recorded these days when the Jews
    turned their enemies back;
    these days when the Jews feasted and
    exchanged their portions.
Queen Esther wrote with full authority to ratify the script of days.
    These days when the *pur* was cast in Israel.
And Mordecai, the dreamer said,
    "All this is God's doing. I remember the dream I had about these
    matters, nothing of which has failed to come true: the little spring
    that became a river, the light that shone, the sun, the flood of
    water. Esther is the river—she whom the king married and made
    queen. The two dragons are Haman and myself. The single nation,
    mine, is Israel, those who cried out to God and were saved. Yes, the
    Lord has saved his people, the Lord has delivered us from all these
    evils, God has worked such signs and great wonders as have never
    happened among the nations."

Yahweh,
As Esther sought your solace for her fear,
   so do I seek comfort in these terrible times.
As Esther heard the death-cries of her people,
   so do I hear the cries of my own time.
As Esther asked you to intervene with saving help,
   so ask I.
As Esther gave her life into your care,
   so do I give my own.
As Esther's actions empowered her people in their struggle,
   so would I act, empowering my people to rise up and reclaim
      Israel.
As Esther blessed her people in your name,
   so do I bless my beloved people in your most powerful name.

My God,
Come to us in this time as you have come before,
And have mercy on me.

REFLECTIONS ON RUTH

In the days of the beloved Ruth
You renewed Israel by a woman's hand.

In faithful caring Ruth left her homeland
    and journeyed with the fair Naomi.

Summoned by love she set aside all that defined her
    and came into a new land.

Summoned by love she left her house of origin
    and became a House of Origin in Bethlehem.

Summoned by love she cast her vow
    from that moment in time
        into all eternity.

On the borders of Judah
They stood alone, together.
Two women
Ruth, the Beloved, said to Naomi, the Fair One,
    "Wherever you go, I will go,
    wherever you live, I will live.
    Your people shall be my people,
    and your God, my God.
    Wherever you die, I will die
    and there I will be buried.
    May Yahweh do this thing to me
    and more also,
    if even death should come between us!"

With these words Ruth betrothed herself to your people, Yahweh.
With these words a foreign woman elected Israel
    and you, Yahweh, she chose for a God.
With these words a widow walked out of Moab and rose up a Matri-
    arch in Judah.
Thus into Bethlehem of Judea came Ruth.
Strength for Noami in this bitter time.
Provider for Naomi in this homeless time.
Gleaner for Naomi in this harvest time.

Now Ruth labored in the barley fields and such was her strength and
demeanor that Boaz, owner of the fields, struck a bargain with
her. He said,
    "My daughter, know this.
    Glean here in my fields.
    Work with my people.
    Watch the reapers and
    gather in their path.
    Here you will work in safety.
    Here you will not know thirst. Only go to my well and the water
        will be drawn for you. Drink and be thirsty no more."
Ruth answered,
    "I come from foreign soil,
    How is it you grant me the bounty of your land?"

He said,
> "Word of your generosity has come to me: all you have done for your mother-in-law, of your journey from the land of your father and mother and the land where you were born to come among a people whom you knew nothing about before you came here. May Yahweh reward you for what you have done! May rich recompense be made to you by Yahweh in whom you have trusted."

And she said,
> "May there be friendship between us.
> Here I have found courage.
> Here I have found kindness.
> Here I have found acceptance."

Boaz and Ruth ate together.
> Bread and wine they shared
>> until they were satisfied.

Ruth labored in the field until evening, then she beat out what she had
> gleaned and with a full basket returned to the waiting Naomi.

The women gave thanks and ate and spoke together.

Naomi instructed Ruth in the ways of her people in that place,
> in that time. And Ruth prepared herself according to Naomi's
> words and she went out.

Coming to the threshing floor of Boaz,
> Biding her time until the proper moment,
> Performing the cultic rhythms of this people, in that place,
>> in that time
> Ruth called forth from Boaz a redeeming kindness.

And Boaz answered, blessing her and saying,
"May Yahweh bless you, my daughter, for this last act you have accomplished is even greater than the first for you have not been frivolous in your choice but have acted with wisdom. Be assured, my kinswoman, I will do whatever you ask, for the people of Bethlehem know your worth."
Boaz went out to secure their agreement in the Law.
When this was done all the people at the gate cried out,
"We are witnesses"; and the elders said,
"May Yahweh make the woman who is to enter your House like Rachel and Leah who together built up the House of Israel.
"Grow mighty in Ephrathah,
Be renowned in Bethlehem."
And thus it was that the exodus of Ruth was fulfilled and she became a woman of promise in Judah.
Ruth and Boaz came together and a child was born.
Obed, a child nursling to the rejoicing Naomi,
celebration of Ruth, adopted of Israel,
father of Jesse, father of David.
David, Man of the hills and of stones.
Man of war and of deep friendships.
Man of lust and of dance.
David, Troubadour King, singing still in our tents.
Betrayed King, hiding among strangers of Israel.
Wandering King, sustained on the Bread of Presence.
David into whose house I come.
I, daughter of Aaron.
Uniting the House of Priests with the House of the Shepherd King.
Remembering you, Ruth, my sister, my mother-in-law, may I be strength in Israel as you are.

Yahweh, God of Israel,
As Ruth loved Naomi,
> so may I love those with whom I join myself.

As Ruth left the house of her parents, the land of her birth to companion a beloved one,
> so may I journey faithfully in the company of my loved ones.

As Ruth spoke her troth to Naomi,
> so may I never withhold words of loving.

As Ruth worked with strength in the harvest,
> so may I work in your vineyard.

As Ruth trusted in you,
> so may I trust.

As Ruth listened to Naomi, her kinswoman,
> so may I listen to those who would impart wisdom to me.

As Ruth went out with boldness to redeem her family according to the custom,
> so would I leave behind timidity and be a woman who claims redemption for Israel.

As Ruth received the blessing of those who witnessed her,
> so would I be blessed by my people.

As Ruth built up the House of Israel like Rachel and like Leah,
> so would I build this House in this time.

Yahweh,
> You are the God who summons.
> You are the God who listens and responds.
> You are the God who comes to those who summon you.
> You are the God in whom people of all lands may find a redeeming home, the God in whom all people may come together.
> Yes, come together in a pledge of trust given on the border between two lands.

You are the God in whom people come together in strength and lawfulness to build a renewed House.
> Sacred as the House of Aaron.
> Mighty as the House of David.
> > Renowned in Bethlehem,
> > > Bethlehem, House of Bread.

Yahweh, God
> Have mercy on me.

REFLECTIONS ON
MIRYAM

My God
Yahweh
Here I am, stilled at the foot of your stoney mountain.
Here I am bent at the mouth of your gaping crevasse.
Here, alone I walk with the lively shadows of Israel,
    with the lively shadows of the dancing, journeying men and
        women of Israel.
Long desert days are but a moment.
Dry desert winds are moist with tears.
Silent desert winds sing out the ancient and future song.
Ages and ages inhabit these very stones:
    braces of the lintel posts; stuff of the tomb-seal;
    water spout in the desert; naked blocks of the altar;
    page of your thumbprint; pillow of Jacob.
    I too, rise limping, rise haunted.
    Broken in freedom.
    Cleansed in Torah.
In the early days of the prophet Miryam
You saved Israel by a woman's hand:
In the days when Israel was slave nation, feared by mighty Egypt,
A people worn down by heavy loads designed to break their strength.

Thoughtful Miryam, the Levite, listened to the edict of Egypt.
Listened to the pharaoh's order to Shiphrah and Puah, Hebrew mid-
    wives.

"When you midwives attend Hebrew women," he said, "watch carefully. If that child is a boy, kill him. If a girl, let her live."

But the midwives were courageous and faithful; they disobeyed the command of the king of Egypt and let the boys live also. So the king of Egypt summoned Shiphrah and Puah, the Hebrew midwives.

"Why," he asked them, "have you done this and spared the boys?" And the women stood tall before him. "The Hebrew women are not like Egyptian women," they answered Pharaoh. "They are hardy and they give birth before the midwife reaches them." God was pleased with the midwives and rejoiced in their strength. The people went on increasing and grew very powerful; as the midwives had reverenced God, God granted them abundance.

Pharaoh then gave his subjects this command:
"Throw all the boys born to the Hebrews into the river, but let the girls live."

Thus the challenge was drawn to raise up in secret the men born in Israel when all Egypt sought to slay them.

When a boy child was born in Miryam's house, they waited to determine the health of the child. When it was seen that he was strong, they conspired to preserve his life. In his early months he was hidden in his mother's care, hushed and hidden in their own household. The family established their daily rhythms in view of the people as though there were no child. As he grew and could be covered in the family quarters no longer, a plan was devised whereby the young Miryam would be the child's protector. The stealthy Miryam by day concealed the baby's camouflaged basket in the wilderness at the river's edge. The cunning Miryam scouted from her sentinel post among the reeds. The militant Miryam maneuvered day by day, evading detection, carefully weaving the hoax which confounded Egypt's people with her subtle deception.

And so it was that Miryam emerged victorious in her campaign to save one Hebrew child, one Levite, one man called Moses—drawn from water—whose name Yahweh would call.

The work of Miryam was auspiciously begun.

In the fullness of their years, it was this Levite family,
    Aaron, Miryam and Moses,
    who centered the Hebrew dream of freedom
    who announced the Hebrew intention to Pharaoh
    who accomplished the Hebrew exodus from Egypt.

As for Miryam, she continued her work: keeping alive the vision of freedom. She and her people were heard by Yahweh. Yahweh witnessed their suffering and their steadfastness. Yahweh inspired the plans of deliverance.

While Moses and Aaron exhibited the power of Yahweh's chosen nation before Pharaoh, the women prepared to establish the treasury of Israel. "Yes, this people will gain such prestige in the eyes of the Egyptians that when you go, you will not go empty-handed. Every woman will seek from her neighbor and her household for silver ornaments and gold and fine clothing and they will be given willingly. With these will the Hebrew nation adorn their sons and daughters. With this action you will plunder the Egyptians."

And so it was according to the plan devised in the Presence of Yahweh, that on that night—so different from all the rest—
Miryam and her Hebrew sisters throughout the nation of Egypt gathered their households behind the blood-smeared doorposts, kneaded the bread of the journey, prepared the holy meal of obedience and lit the candle of watching each in her own home.
Miryam and her Hebrew sisters gathered their tribe for the journey, packed their households for the journey, centered their minds for the journey.
Miryam and her Hebrew sisters rose up in the morning and plundered Egypt according to their plan; adorned their sons and daughters with the treasure of Egypt and went out with their armed men following the vibrant Shadow of Yahweh into the wilderness.
It was this trail of awesome events that led the people Israel through the wasteland of Egypt to the netherside of the Sea of Reeds and here they gave thanks. Moses and Aaron and the sons of Israel sang songs in honor of Yahweh. Miryam, the prophet, took up the timbrel and all the women of Israel followed her with timbrels dancing and singing:

"Singing the songs of triumph.
Singing the songs of the triumphant people of Yahweh.
Yahweh, Triumphant One, Singer of our Songs."

Their song ended,
    their first flight done
    the people placed one foot before the other and came into your
       wilderness. Wrenched from the sweetness of slavery, they tasted
       the bitter root of your freedom, Yahweh.
Then, as now,
    they learned as I now learn,
    who you are.
    In your presence the stones rise up and quench our thirst.
    In your presence the dew is bread which today is and tomorrow is
       spoilt.
    In your hearing is our complaint.
    In your hearing is our thanksgiving.
In the torment of Meribah, we threaten to stone your chosen one.
In the refreshment of Meribah, water pours from the rock at your feet,
    touched by your chosen one, and we drink.
    Here, Adonai, were we given Torah.
    Here, we were given Shabbot.
    Here, borne on eagles' wings you have brought us to yourself.
    Here, in you, in our obedient embrace of your covenant, we have
       become a nation which is yours in the midst of an earth filled
       with nations that belong to you.
    And we are counted as a nation of priests, a consecrated nation.
    Here, you have known us by name and promised to show us your
       way.

And here you requested of this people a gift. You directed Moses to say to this people how the gift might be given: the first Temple built in which this people would be born into a new Law.

Eagerly, Miryam the prophet listened as her brother, Moses the Levite, spoke to the whole community of Israel. The light of Yahweh, the Creative One, the God Who Is, shone within the community and the community poured forth its treasure. From those who were prompted in their heart came forth the plunder of Egypt, their newly won treasure.

They came, men and women all giving willingly, bringing brooches, rings, bracelets, gold of every kind.

They came, men and women all giving willingly, bringing purple stuffs of violet shade or red, crimson stuffs, fine linen, skins dyed red and fine leather.

They came, men and women all giving willingly, bringing silver, bronze and acacia wood.

All the skilled women set their hands to spinning. All the women and men willingly used their special talents.

Did we not bring more than enough?
Did we not teach one another our skills?
Did we not—each of us—
    embroiderer, dyer, cutter of stones,
    engraver, weaver, spinner of linen,
    carpenter, carver, setter of gems,
    surpass all our previous artistry?
Were we not filled with the spirit of God, in wisdom, in understand-
        ing, in knowledge and in all manner of workmanship?
Did we not stain a new blue, a new scarlet and entwine a new linen
        more original, more cunning than we had ever done before?
Were not our hands and our minds enlivened nearly to excess?
Till you, Yahweh, cried out,
    "Enough!"
Our abundance spawned in you was sufficient for all the work of that
        time and was too much.
From this outpouring of gifts was assembled—
    The Holy Place, The Tabernacle, The Tent of Meeting.
From this outpouring of Spirit was built—
    An Ark, wood and gold, womb of your Word.
From this outpouring of Spirit was born a witness, a living testimony
        of one people's natal moment,
    one people caressed in the palm of your hand.
You anointed Aaron and his House.

You instructed Aaron and his House.
>Make yourselves holy—for Yahweh is your God.
>Listen and accomplish what is given—for Yahweh is your God.
>Feed the poor from your harvest—for Yahweh is your God.

You entrusted your work to Aaron and his House.
>Whenever the Tabernacle is moved—the Levites are to dismantle it.
>Whenever the Tabernacle is set up—the Levites are to rebuild it.
>The Levites are to be responsible to the Tabernacle of Testimony.

Aaron and his House have been elected from Israel to be Yahweh's own.
>They shall now and forever pitch their tent in the midst of this people that they may furnish the Tent of Meeting; that they may service your Word; that they may live as the dedicated ones.

It is written also from that time: "If a man or a woman shall separate themselves to vow a vow of a Nazarite, to separate themselves unto God they shall abide by the Nazarite pledges. Throughout the whole of their days of their Nazarite this one is a person consecrated to Yahweh."

In their long journey in the desert Moses reached out from Israel to another tribe and brought into his own family an Ethiopian woman for a wife. He blended the seed of Israel and the blood of Ethiopia. His own were enraged and confronted him. Righteous Miryam, the prophet, with her brother Aaron saw what Moses, their brother, had done. Their racist pride rose in them, spewed from their mouths and they admonished Moses saying, "Do you think God speaks through you alone? We too, can speak with authority." The three went into the Tent of Meeting to seek accord. Here in the Tent of Meeting they sought meaning from Yahweh. The prophet Miryam was re-formed. She came to know that as God's prophet she was required to speak from the depths of her prayer, from God's visions, from the clarity of her dreams, and never again from the stagnant reservoir of custom or the sterile page of law on which the ink of God had dried. She learned that the prophet's work was not to spill the bitter gall of habituated tradition on the people of God, but instead to seek into God's vision and draw clear and stark God's living word for humankind. And she was taught that from time to time God would speak to some people directly, without a veil. Speak with such clarity that no doubt would cloud their action and this one to whom God spoke directly would proceed directly in all innocence. God alone is the reference point. God's law is often confounding but eternally new.

The three arose and came out of the Tent of Meeting. The humbled Miryam, God's prophet, stood before Israel as a sign of one rebuked. Miryam became leprous, white as snow, and Aaron looked upon Miryam, and behold, she was a leper.

Aaron cried out to Moses, "My leader, such a price for a moment of foolishness! Let her not be so accursed!" and Moses cried out to Yahweh, "O God, I plead with you, heal her."

Through the penitent Miryam's pain Yahweh taught all Israel the full import of the lives and words of those called to be prophets, those called to be priests in Israel, called to live Torah. Miryam went out from Israel. Seven days and seven nights, prophecy and priesthood agonized in exile. The prophet of God wandered in lonely pain outside the camp. And the people journeyed not until it was over and the beloved Miryam was restored again.

From that time until this and forever God's people know that the House of Levi, the sons and daughters of Aaron bear a special sign. As prophet, priest and shepherd we go daily to the well of Yahweh. We mold our sight to the vision of Yahweh. We pray in listening to the mind of Yahweh and we speak not that which comes from petrified minds and hackneyed customs. We speak that which comes from God.

The journey continued and near the end of it your prophet Miryam died and was buried in the desert. There also her brother Aaron died and her brother Moses died. Priests dead in the desert. Struggling, wrestling midwives of Israel, dead in the desert. Their journey remembered in us. Their journey continued in our time.

Yahweh,
Hear my cry.
As Miryam saw her people captive,
    so do I see my people.
As Miryam stepped forth to be a liberator in Israel,
    so would I be a part of our liberation.
As Miryam was a woman of strength for her Hebrew sisters,
    so would I be strong.
As Miryam knew herself to be a daughter of Levi,
    so do I know that my kinswoman Elizabeth and I are of that
       priestly House.
As Miryam struggled to keep your Law with her heart and her
       prophecy,
    so do I struggle to know your way.
As Miryam received your blessing in the desert,
    so bless me here, Yahweh, my only One.

My God
Bless me and keep me.
Let your face shine upon me and be gracious to me.
Yahweh, uncover your face to me and bring me shalom.

My God
Yahweh
God Who Shatters War
Come pitch your tent in the midst of your people.
Remember, O Saving One,
Reveal yourself in the time of our distress.
As for me, give me courage.

The wisdom of Deborah stands firm in my memory and I who love you
        would be like the sun arising in strength.

The courage of Judith sings a new song to you, O God,
for you spoke and things came into being:
you sent your breath and they were put together
and no one can resist your voice.

The trusting obedience of Esther stirs in my heart,
and you know that your handmaid finds pleasure only in you,
God of Abraham and God of Sarah.

The remarkable loving of Ruth enlivens my search,
and I too would betroth myself to those who choose you:
to live as they live,
to die as they die,
to worship together forever.

The lifelong dedication of Miryam calls me to new commitment.
        Miryam, my namesake, with you I would pitch my tent in the midst
        of the people that I may furnish the Tent of Meeting with
        a witness of the Holy Word.

My God
Yahweh
Your strength does not lie in numbers
    nor your might in violent men,
God, all mighty and all powerful, in your creative wisdom are we
        victorious.

Miryam arose and went out of the desert.
She put away the sackcloth dress,
    washed her body and her hair.
In the simple clothing of her people Miryam adorned herself
    and she returned home.
Peace walked with her.
In common work she spent her days.
Inner spaces open,
    undefended,
        she waited on her God.

The Prayer of Miryam in Jerusalem During the Lifetime of Jesus

ANNUNCIATION

Luke 1:26-38

In those days when the people of Judea were oppressed
    in the reign of King Herod
    in the town of Nazareth there was a woman named Miryam.

In prayer Miryam watched.
Eyes of her soul turned inward, she watched.
Ears of her spirit stretched out, she watched.
Watched for Yahweh in stillness.

In awe Miryam listened.
With the firm beat of her heart, she listened.
With the deep stroke of her breath, she listened.
Listened for Yahweh in stillness.

In the stillness Miryam reached out.
Mind alive, she reached out.
Memory reflecting, she reached out.
Inviting her God to inspire.

The Shadow streamed into her being.
Greeting the core of her soul.
Hearing, she stretched for the life source.
Embracing the quickening call.

"How is this? I know not!" she responded.
Stumbling in God's desert of time.
"But you speak and all things come together.
I will
     as you say
         let it be."

Her lifetime of shadowy knowing was
      confirmed in the quieting joy.
Summoning cadences, ancient and deep,
      echoed the call of God's peace.

Miryam arose and went out.
Holding the knowledge of change, went out.
Accepting the newness of challenge, went out.
Went out to begin the task.

Miryam embarked on the journey.
Her mind precise for the journey.
Her soul enflamed for the journey.
Journeyed to the arms of Elizabeth.

In the warmth of those arms, she knew.
Ancient pathways op'ning before her, she knew
Words of her people streamed from her mouth, she knew.
Knew that her God lived within her.

MAGNIFICAT OF ACCEPTANCE

Luke 1:38

My soul trembles in the presence of the loving Creator
    and my spirit prepares itself to walk hand in hand
    with the God who saves Israel
    because I have been accepted by God
    as a simple helpmate.
Yes, forever in the life of humankind
    people will sing of this loving encounter;
    through remembering this moment, the faithful
    will know all things are possible in God.
Holy is the place within me where God lives.
God's tender fingers reach out from age to age
    to touch the softened inner spaces of those
    who open their souls in hope.
I have experienced the creative power of God's embracing arms
    and I know the cleansing fire of unconditional love.
I am freed from all earthly authority
    and know my bonding to the Author of all earthly things.

I am filled with the news of good things;
    my favor with God,
    faithful trust in the gentle shadow of the Most High,
    the mystery of my son, Jesus,
    the gift of companionship with my beloved kinswoman,
        Elizabeth, who believes as I believe.
The place in my heart that I had filled
    with thoughts of fear and inadequacy
    has been emptied and I am quiet within.

God comes to save Israel, our holy family,
remembering that we are the ones who remember,
    . . . according to the kinship we have known . . .
    remembering that we are the ones who remember
    and that where God and people trust each other
    there is home.

Magnificat of Friendship

Luke 1:39-56

My soul flowers in the light of your love, my God,
    and my spirit sings Alleluia in the reality of your joyful presence,
        because you have chosen my kinswoman and me with the
        summons of your eyes.
Yes, we are known now and for all time. We are known as women,
    blessed.
Holy is your name.
The tenderness of your hand rests on us as we journey in your way.
Your power in my life has led me into the embrace of loving arms.
You have exposed my lonely pride that I might turn my head to your
      nurturing breast.
You have revealed the hollowness of achievements and have opened in
      my heart a space filled with simple, loving moments.
My hunger you have satisfied,
    my excess you have ignored.
You are my help as I remember your tender love for me,
    . . . for we have touched each other you and I
    and we have made promises. . . .
I remember your tenderness for all that you have begun in me
    and in those with whom I walk
    and I respond with all that I am becoming
    in this hour and in all times to come.

MAGNIFICAT
FOR A DREAMER

Matthew 1:18-22

My soul is grateful for your tender caring
    and my spirit rejoices in you, God, my provider,
    because you have given an enabling dream
    to a person that I love.
Yes, now we both know the blessedness
    of our life together,
    for the Almighty has shown us clearly
    the rightness of the path ahead.
Holy is the name of the One who speaks in dreams:
    Clarifying visions reach from age to age
    into the sleep of people who seek to know their own way.
God has shown the freeing power of an inner answer
    to one who asks in genuine yearning,
    "What shall I do in this moment, Yahweh?"
    God leaves unanswered those who twist and construe
    each jot and tittle of the law to insure their future.

God has brushed aside the authoritative hand
     of those who would lay upon our heads
     their narrow reading of the Law,
     and touched with a revealing kiss
     the sleeping brow of my beloved.
The searching ones have been filled with holy knowing,
     others will lift their eyebrows
     in idle speculation at the firmness of our step.

God has come in vivid imagery
     to the help of my companion and my self,
     remembering God is a dreamer,
     . . . according to the dreams our Creator dreamed in the begin-
       ning
     that there would be a people who loved enough
     to follow the beckoning heart of the Lonely One . . .
     remembering God is a dreamer
     who never leaves us to walk the pathway alone.

Magnificat of Waiting for the Fullness of Time

Luke 1:56

My soul reflects quietly on your fullness,
    and my spirit grows stronger in the hope of your promise,
    God my redeemer, because you have filled me with the
    knowing that you are alive within me.
Yes, day by day through the course of time
    my awareness of the call to blessed fulfillment increases
    for you have done great things in me.
Holy is this time,
    and patience is your gift
    to all who nurture the seed of your love.
You have changed my life;
    I was so confident in my unknowing.
You have deflected my fervent thrust toward iron-clad goals,
    and spread before me your vision of fragile simplicity.
My longing to be a healing and reconciling person to your people
    is affirmed within the daily comings and goings of my life;
    my illusions of my own wholeness are mercifully revealed.

You are here now in this seeming emptiness of waiting,
    remembering your intent,
        . . . according to the promise made in the beginning of time . . .
    remembering your intent to reach through the work of my life
    that your fullness may be known now, in our time.

Magnificat of the Stable

Luke 2:6-7

My soul rests confidently in the animal warmth
    and the lantern light of this simple place, Yahweh,
    and my spirit rejoices in the privacy of this time of birthing
    we share with you, O God of Creation,
    for you come alive again tonight
    in the blood and water of your people.
Yes, this is the time we have waited for.
    This is the moment of blessing.
Holy is birth,
    and you shall show yourself from age to age
    in those who enter into creation with you.
You have shown the power of a dream enfleshed
    and we are humbled.
You have pulled down all our strivings
    and lifted up this simple, common moment.
This stable is filled with good things,
    new life and happy people.
    Are those in the inn rooms as satisfied?
You have come to Israel,
    mindful of our shared nature,
    . . . according to the promise of Eden . . .
    mindful of our nature to seek the wisdom of new life together
    as long as we walk the earth.

Magnificat of the Shepherds

Luke 2:15-20

My soul delights in the greatness of the people summoned by angels,
    and my spirit embraces each puzzled face that peers through the
      lamplight at the warm-bundled gift of our song-filled God.
    As our eyes meet, joy flows between us
    and our chins are lifted with gladness.
Yes, from this day forward
    all generations shall raise their voices
    to proclaim those who gather here as blessed,
    for the Almighty has done great things for us.
Holy are the simple people.
    And God's mercy reaches from age to age
    for those who would join hands and follow a holy calling.
The power of wonder has called them from the meadows;
    they are no longer cold.
Kings sit alone in their palaces,
    and we laugh together
    in this comfortable place.
In the midst of this night
    we have shared the bread and meat of our haversacks
    and our wineskins pass from mouth to mouth.
    The kitchen of the inn is long locked and shuttered.

Come, God of Israel, celebrate with your people,
    mindful of your love of dancing,
    . . . according to the stories of David and of Judith . . .
    mindful of your love of dancing,
    with garlands of straw flowerlets wound about our necks,
    with the bells of the flock and tongue-licked pans for tambou-
      rines,
    we celebrate in psalm and canticle.

Maranatha

    Maranatha

      Maranatha

MAGNIFICAT OF THE MAGI

Matthew 2:1-12

I am immersed in peaceful silence in the presence
   of those you lead to us, my God.
      With quiet awe my spirit listens to the story of the star-led quest
         for this newly born one.
      I feel your knowing eyes probing the depths of my wonder-filled
         heart, and my heart responds in the fullness of knowing.
Yes, this day of recognition, affirmed by wise people,
      shall be remembered as long as stars shine,
         for in this time the Almighty has become a simple child through us,
         the ones who have united with you to claim your promised presence.
Holy is this child's name,
      and caring shall flow from age to age
      among those who touch our lives.
He lifts his tiny hand to these mighty rulers,
      and they understand pure power.
Their prideful eyes are washed clean with tears.
These Magi have disregarded Herod
      and bow before our little child.
Their hearts overflow with the fruit of their search,
      and their rich gifts lie in shadow on the floor.

You have come yourself to Bethlehem, Yahweh,
        mindful of our trust and your love for your people.
        . . . according to the promise told by Isaiah . . .
        mindful of the trust those who love you have shared from
        our parents Sarah and Abraham and their descendants
        as numerous and eternal as the stars.

Magnificat of Freedom

Luke 2:41

My soul sings a thankful song to you, my God,
    Creator of the Universe,
    who blesses the fruit of the vine.
    And my spirit rejoices in the company of a grateful people
    because of what you did for me
    when I came out of Egypt.
Yes, in joyful obedience
    we remember the day we went forth from Egypt
    all the days of our lives.
    We went forth that we might come into the land
    that you have promised us.
Holy is your name,
    and from age to age
    your voice is heard calling in the land . . .
    calling to those who say they would be free.
You have shown us the power of a yearning spirit,
    you have turned your back on the self-sufficient.
Pharaoh weeps for Egypt's first-born,
    and Israel's legacy lives on.
Tonight your people feast upon the lamb.
    Together we eat the food of freedom
    and spill the wine for those who suffer injustice
    in the cause of freedom.

You, God of Creation, have come to the help of your servant, Israel,
    mindful of our covenant with you,
    . . . according to the teachings of Moses . . .
    mindful of the covenant we share with you,
    on this night so different from all the rest,
    we celebrate
    now and forever in Jerusalem.

Magnificat of Now

John 2:1-12

My spirit watches for the potent moment, Yahweh,
   and in the midst of this celebration
   you are a throbbing presence.
   All of us are here.
   All of us are ready.
Yes, in this time the nearness of your blessing is felt.
   "Wine they have not," I said to him.
   "What is this to me and thee," he said.
   "Not yet has come my hour."
Holy is this work now beginning.
   Blessed is the first step.
   Blessed are those who, prepared,
     have the courage to begin.
   Blessed are you, Yahweh, the enabler of deeds
     great and simple for these people today.
The fruit of this work offers nourishment to generation after gener-
   ation for those who harvest it.

You show us the potency of people with a clear commitment;
    you scatter the energies of those who vacillate.
You remove the moderators and the intercessors;
    you speak directly to those who speak to you.
You provide answers for those who question;
    to those who know the answers, you are silent.

You are here now, the Available One,
    for the work of these times,
    mindful of your continuing newness
    . . . according to the traditions of all searching people . . .
    mindful of the continuing newness of each one of us,
    we come with open minds
    to accomplish the work of this day.

MAGNIFICAT OF UNDERSTANDING

Luke 8:19-21

I am a witness to the work of God and today my hope has been gratified.

We are now brought together as one family by the words of our Rabbi with all others who hear the word of God and do it.

Today we came to search for him as he taught, and he spoke from their midst saying to us and to them, "Mother of mine and brothers of mine, these are the ones hearing and doing the word of God." The spark of holy recognition ignited between us and even among those who listened and heard.

Yes, from this day forward all generations shall know that each one of us stands with God and with one another in holy relationship. The Almighty has released new energies of loving in us.

Blessed are we.

Holy is the name of the One who teaches us
and whose understanding enriches the bonding
of those who choose to live as God's family.

Yahweh has empowered us all to motherhood and fatherhood,
    to sisterhood and brotherhood,
    and has exposed our insensitivity to each other.
God has freely given us equally each to the other
    and has not asked that we be worthy of this gift.
God has filled our moments with the tender knowing of how very
    dear we are to each other.
    Those who assume authority over the ways of another
    are sent off to ponder their loneliness.

God has come to clarify Israel, the beloved,
    knowing the depths of our potential,
    . . . according to the promise made to our ancestors . . .
    the promise that Israel's God is One God
    and in this Holy Oneness
    we are one.

Magnificat of Reconciliation

Luke 4:14-30

My soul rejoices in you, Yahweh,
  and my spirit dances within your presence, my God,
  because you who love mightily look upon me,
  one who stands with arms stretched out toward you.
From this day and forever all who come to life,
  one after one, shall remember me and shall pray,
  "Blessed are we when we open our hearts and
  receive in joy the seed of the Everlasting One."
Holy is your name.
You are the gentle one who reaches out in tenderness
  from age to age
  to caress with your hand the heads of those
  who bend their necks.
With powerful arms you embrace each of us.

The proud hearts that we hold out to you,
    you break and scatter.
You pull down the structures and fantasies with which we fortify
      ourselves,
    and you teach us the simple things.
When we are hungry you fill us with good things.
    When we are glutted you teach us patience
    that we may come hungry again to your table.

This day and forever you stand with your people,
    those who remember your tenderness,
    . . . having given us your word, your promise . . .
    we remember your tenderness as we walk in safety.
    For you are Yahweh
    in whom we trust.

Magnificat of Conversion

John 12:35-37

My soul comes in the darkness of unknowing
    to the secret room of Yahweh;
    my spirit seeks understanding
    in the happenings of these days,
    because God looks upon the people in a new way.
Yes, from this day forward
    all generations will speak of these strange events
    as wonderful;
    and those of us who walk blindly trusting
    will be called blessed,
    for the presence of the Almighty, the Most Loving One,
    is felt in our land.
Holy is the name of the One who is eternally new.
    God's guiding hand reaches
    from age to age
    for those who grope and stumble
    in search of the saving way.
We are shown the power of touching
    and simply being open to each other;
    our proud imaginings of the high place
    of our chosen nation are scattered and ground down.

The warrior-king we expected to establish us on earth
    as uncontested righteous power has not come,
    and we see instead the promised messenger
    with dusty feet and hidden words.
The hungry of heart are fed with enabling love.
    In places where there was need people now give to others
    from their abundance.
    The rich are troubled and rumble of revenge.

You have come, Yahweh, because we have summoned you to help us.
    Remember in your mercy that we are often confused by freedom.
    . . . according to our history we are the ones who wandered
    doubting and angry on the Sinai journey,
    choosers of gold and wantonness
    in our fear of your inadequacy . . .
    remember in your mercy that we are often confused by freedom
    and turn us around until we stand with clarity
    on the holy ground you have prepared for us.
    Help us to trust the fragility of each human heart.
    Help us to empower with simplicity the one-by-oneness
    you have taught us,
    for we are the struggling, longing people
    stumbling and striding in your shadowy desert
    brothers and sisters to Miryam and Aaron,
    seeking our homeland in you.

Magnificat of the People Who Gather at the Temple

Luke 21:37-38

My soul opens before you, O God.
> All that I am becomes acceptable in your saving love
> because you have asked me to look within myself
> with searching eyes.

Yes, from now on
> I know that I am truly blessed
> for you have helped me to do the difficult things.

Holy is your name.

Your mercy reaches into the hearts of all people
> who seek inner knowing.

You are the Empowering One.

In your presence I can face my own darkness.

You have annihilated the fear that made of my spirit a fortress
> and have led me to my true self . . . open and undefended
> I walk beside the living waters of my soul in peace.

You are my bread. My hunger for life and loving is satisfied
> when I am in your presence
> and in the presence of those who know you.

People who come to our gatherings
    not accepting your love for themselves
    look upon our fullness with puzzlement
    and leave shaking their heads.

You, most gentle counsellor . . . beloved rabbi,
    come into the life of each person who invites you.
    You come with compassion
    . . . remembering the tears we have shed together . . .
    you come with compassion
    as you have always come
    and as you will come in future days.

Magnificat of Prophecy

Luke 21:31-38

Jerusalem leaps with joy in the knowing of God
    and the core of the universe exults in the Creative One
    because this One has looked upon us with love.
Yes, from this day forward all people
    now and to come
    will be enriched by our choices
    for the Fertile Lover sows in each one of us
    a holy possibility.
Holy is the name of God,
    and embracing all time and space,
    this Gentle One nurtures those who cherish life
    and hope with open hearts.
Power resides in this One Alone,
    and in no other.
In places where pride and arrogance corrupt God's work,
    a praying people will seek wisdom
    and act with discernment
    destroying the illusion of might.

There is but one Law.
     All pretenders will be driven out
     that the way may be made clear
     for the feet of the simple ones.
There is nourishment in Jerusalem
     for those who hunger for peace and fairness.
     For those who take more than their part,
     from them shall all real food be hidden
     and they shall lie gasping in their worthless largess.

God will walk with each one of us who quietly reaches out,
     mindful of intimate devotion and courage
     . . . for there are whispered promises between us . . .
     mindful of the intimate devotion and courage in knowing God
     we walk in caring with all people, all creation,
     and in this Truth
     Jerusalem will live forever.

Magnificat of Desolation

John 19:17-19

My soul seeks out Yahweh in the secret places of my heart,
    my spirit roams the empty spaces of my prayer, sighing,
    "My savior . . . my savior.
    I am forsaken and cast down.
    Will there be a tomorrow?
    Will there be generations to come who call the name of Yahweh?
    What does it mean to be called blessed?
    Why does the Almighty stand aside now in these hard times?"

Hidden is the face of God.
Concealed the mercy which has flowed
    from age to age.
I am afraid.

The strong ones of Yahweh are routed and scattered,
    the arms of the proud have struck with power.
The prince of Yahweh's promise
    is pulled down beneath his crushing burden;
    he is pressed onto the tree
    and lifted up beyond our comforting,
    and the oppressors walk with a light step,
    jesting among themselves, mindless of our pain.
The hungry are without desire,
    and they regret having eaten at your table;
    the rich consume the food of God's people.

Where are you who never desert those who seek you?
    remembering you are our stronghold
    . . . according to the promise you have made to me, your help-
        mate, and to your faithful ones . . .
    remembering you are our stronghold when times are hard.
    Come back, Yahweh, rescue us!
    Save us if you love us,
    for in death there is no remembrance of you;
    who can sing your praises in Sheol?

Magnificat of Grief

John 19:40-42

I come to you, Adonai
    because you wait for me.
    I know that at daybreak
    you will listen for my voice
    and at dawn I will hold myself in readiness for you,
    because you are the one I have relied upon.

Yes, from this day forward
    I am alone,
    and all generations will call me
    the one who sorrows,
    for the Almighty has asked great things from me.

I do not understand the way of the Holy One.
    Your mercy seems far away
    and present only in the memory of our people.

I am brought low by the power of this moment.
    My confidence in you,
    my sureness of what is just,
    is confounded.

You have allowed my beloved to die.
    People in the town go about this evening of preparation
    as though it was just the same as any other evening.

My mind and my spirit are hungry
    for the nourishment that only the presence
    of my lost love could give.
    I watch others from a distance
    feeding on the touch of their families
    and I hunger more.

Listen to my cry for help, my hope and my God,
    remember how you have loved me
    . . . according to the promises you made
    in that simple love-filled stable room
    so long ago . . .
    remember how you have loved me
    and touch me again.

103

MAGNIFICAT OF RESURRECTION

John 20:19-21

My soul sings and
    my spirit delights and rejoices,
    O Faithful God,
    because you have removed the stone which was
    rolled over our hearts and
    we are risen.

Yes, from this day forward all generations
    will call us blessed
    for the Almighty has called us forth from death
    and we have responded.

Holy is the name of God,
    and compassion reaches from age to age
    for those who walk hand in hand
    with the Everlasting One.

You have shown power over death.
    You have humiliated those who believed
    they could destroy your living Word.

You have enfeebled those who would rule by their own might and
     empowered the simple people who trust in you,
     O God who creates and companions.

The anguished of heart are stilled and
     made whole again by this good news,
     and the arrogant are reduced to eternal confusion.

You have come to the help of Israel, your faithful one,
     Israel who remembers you are the God who saves,
     . . . according to the history of our time with you . . .
     Israel who remembers you are the God who saves us from bond-
       age,
     from faithlessness,
     and from ultimate violence.
     You are the Forever Living One,
     the Shatterer of Death.

The Prayer of Miryam in the Jerusalem of the Resurrection Community

In those days when the people of Judea were oppressed
in the reign of King Herod there was a woman named Miryam.

Miryam of the changing way.
Aging, growing, becoming.
She left her home to root herself
    in the security of God.

Woman of beginnings and endings,
    celebrating and mourning,
    living events of brutal desolation
    with faithful witness to the mysterious way.

Woman of Yahweh's chosen nation,
    leading her few companions to the historic turning point . . .
    founding mother of God's nationless ones.

Woman of authentic presence,
    initiating
    participating
    claiming to the full her prayer-drawn vision
    grounded in reality.

Sustaining and supporting with her knowledge
    and the depth of her faith
    those whose role was different from her own;
    accepting and embracing her companions
    called equally with her to share the founding work.

Miryam who lived in Jerusalem
    during the Eden-time of the Resurrected One;
    the healing, softening, ripening time
    of the Loving Shadow cast upon their moments and their days;
    the bonding-time of people who had chosen
      to daily break the bread with their own hands
      and pass the cup among them;
    the birthing-time of searching and formation,
    the time we dare not let slip away
    from current vital recollection
    lest we forget the essence of our own identity.

ASCENSION MORNING

Acts 1:1-11

"Why do you stand there looking into the sky?"

Because my eyes are clinging to the swirling morning mist
    that has enveloped him . . .
    the risen one . . . the Christ.

Because my ears are searching in the gusty wind
    for one more word to ground me here . . .
    a word of firmament . . . a holding sound.

Because my heart is sailing high in the whipping breeze
    dodging and dancing with my heart of hearts . .
    and I am heartless . . . for the moment.

"Why do you stand there looking into the sky?"

Because the sky has taken him away.
    Will he not come again from just such a sky?
    Is it not right that I keep watch?

Here would I stay forever,
    fasting, praising constantly,
    eyes fixed upon the heavens
    just to catch a glimpse of him.

What if the cloud should part
      and no one was here to greet the Christ?

What if God should look again for one still spirit
      to receive a word and I am busy elsewhere?

I would remain fixed in this moment,
      in this place.
      I would capture forever the feeling and hold it like a flickering oil
         lamp in my cupped hands.
      Guarding the place, and the light, and the moment,
      I have a purpose.
      I am relieved from daily living in uncertainty.

"Why do you stand there looking into the sky?

Yes, why?

Why do I stand here looking at the sky?
      It is a blue and quiet sky,
      no longer teeming with the ferment of my longing.

I am alone, gone are the others.
They know I often choose to be alone.
I need this time to store away the treasure of the moment,
      a time for pondering.

111

But now the sun is hot and hunger gnaws at me.
The voices of companions grow distant and I would be with them.
We have walked the long way together and we are somehow essential
            to each other.

I leave this place to you, Asker of Questions,
Watch it with care.

The moment and the feeling
        I will take with me and
        share with those I meet along the way.
        And in the sharing I will return in heart and mind
        bringing with me others who will watch a while with you.

As for me, I long to slip my hand into the hand of my brother,
        to feel my sister's arm around my waist.
        My feet would pound the earth
        gathering dust with other sandaled feet
        feeling cool and water-washed at the end of our day's journey.
        My mouth is hungry for the warm wine and
        sharing words and kisses of my new-formed family.

Knowing I cannot stay with you
    I will take you with me.

Alive and thriving
    I will daily gather in the enveloping mist and place it in the midst
        of us.

Stay hidden, Rabboni, if that is your way.
    See how long you can resist our company,
    our silence, our prayer,
    our festival, our work,
    our dance, and the deep joy of our embracing.

You in our moments,
    we in you,
    the risen one
        the Christ.

A Meeting

Acts 1:13-26

Today we gather.
Meeting together to consider
    where we stand
    and who we are.

We come to order ourselves
    into a new sense of order according to our progress
    from the last gathering to this one.

Be with us, O God,
    in this space and time
    as we affirm and shape the changes
    in our understanding of the Way.

We desire not to fly apart
    in garish fantasy of vision
    but rather to move the boundaries
    that we have set before
    in order to encompass and embrace
    the living and breathing growth
    of each and all.

We work in prayer and dialogue.
   In going back to see where we have been,
   we steady ourselves
   for the journey forward today.

We are here
   to reconcile all that we were,
      our trust . . . our hopelessness
      our joy . . . our despair
      our confirming . . . our betrayal
   to offer a farewell to those departed
   and to welcome those who are newly come.
   To confess, absolve, reconcile, renew.
   To be all that we can be.
To set firm a pathway that is possible.
   Possible for us to walk until we meet again
   to reassess the journey
   and again set firm a pathway.

Each step along the way we clear the stones and obstacles,
   healing and refreshing each other.
   We listen openly to each tale of travel and
   hear each one's proposal for the time ahead.

Knowing you are here, God,
    we are freer in our interaction,
    more daring in the sharing of our personal visions,
    loving in our confrontation,
    deeply silent in consideration and
    accepting in the choices that for a little while will help us to define
      our actions
    until broader definitions draw us on.

In this your presence,
    we meet to order ourselves anew,
    to consider where we stand and who we are.
Today we gather.

PENTECOST

Acts 2:1-21

Here I am, Yahweh,
    afire with some unnamed energy.

Today was just a common day.
After early prayer and eating
    we met together in one room.
The quiet was so deep,
    my mind stilled,
    supported by the sturdiness of our silence.

Suddenly, we heard a rushing sound,
    as being born of a wind.
    Violent, it filled the house where we were sitting.
    There appeared to us scattered tongues of a fire,
    which alighted on each one of us.
In awe we watched,
    and now
Here I am, Yahweh,
    afire with some unnamed energy.

This moment was just a common moment.
I am often stilled and strengthened by our prayer.
The chanting fills my throat with resonant balm
    and my ears channel the ancient melodies
    to calm my stirring mind.
    Times of quiet breathing are a symphony.
    Words of sharing feed my soul.
We sit in bodily harmony
    and sense that we are more together than we are each alone.
    Today, in time-suspended sitting,
    like a seasoned log cast upon the reddened coals
    unwatched and dormant,
    I suddenly burst into flames.
Here I am, Yahweh,
    afire with some unnamed energy.

This time becomes the common time.
As I look up and dare to gaze at those here gathered,
    I see the spirit shared.
Each sister's eyes aglow with wondrous infusion
    and color high upon the bearded brothers' cheeks.

I see you, my companions!
I see you in all that it means to see.
    In that flaming recognition we ignite in sounds and syllables
    synonymous with utterings of devoted people everywhere,
    who, like ourselves,
    sing and sigh in consonance with God.

And I, so aging and respected,
I, so simple in my speech,
I, Miryam
    am in the midst of us as we spill out into the street.
    Speaking the tongues of many!
    Amazing and most wonderful!
    Chattering as though over-filled with sweet wine!
    A spirit effervescent, almost o'er done,
Until I cried, "Enough! Yahweh, enough!"

Here I am, Yahweh,
    afire with some unnamed energy.

This fiery fervor I bequeath to common people
    everywhere and for all time.
I give you sturdy, strengthening prayer together,
    supported and sustained by chanted rhythms and ancient sounds;
    deepened and united in harmonious breathing and shared still-
        ness;
    exchanging words and gazes,
    open, faithful, undefended
    until like seasoned logs
    cast upon the reddened coals of your inheritance,
    unwatched and dormant,
    your spirits conflagrate.

I give you common songs to sing and dances,
    laughter, tears and kisses.

I give you people who will watch in wonder
    at the sight of the bonding of your spirits.
    Who will weep in loneliness as they witness the holy fire
    that welds you to each other.

I give you eternal words to open your gentle glowing hearts
as you go out to meet the iron bands of fear and dogma.
Witness to the searching faithfully.
Warm the people. Pitch your tent in the midst of them.
Nurture the fire.
Make space in the prayer circle.
Embrace the lonely.
Incorporate the peaceful Way.
Journey in the deserts of your time.
Know yourself and your company of special people.
Lay your hands upon each other
    that each may know the resurrecting way,
    that each may cry in joy.
Here I am, Yahweh,
    afire with an unnamed energy.

Dormition

In those days when the people of Jesus were free
in the reign of the Spirit
in the city of Jerusalem there was a woman named Miryam.

In wonder Miryam watched
Witnesses healing, teaching, restoring,
Gamaliel's counsel prophetic.
Watched the glory of Judah.

In joy Miryam listened—
Men and women willingly bringing
all their possessions, now common wealth.
Listened to the churning of freedom.

In gratitude Miryam knew—
Shaken the Spirit; anchored the cornerstone
Houses made holy in meeting.
Knew that her God was enlivened.

A shadow slipped into her being,
greeting the core of her soul.
Hearing she stretched for the life-source
Embracing the quickening call.

"How is this? I know not!" she responded.
Stumbling in God's desert of time.
"But you speak and all things come together.
I will
        as you say
                let it be."

Her lifetime of shadowy knowing was
        confirmed in the quieting joy.
Summoning cadences, ancient and deep,
        echoed the call of God's peace.

Miryam, aware, reached out.
Holding the knowledge of change, reached out.
Accepting the newness of challenge, reached out.
Reached out to begin the renewing.

Miryam embarked on the journey.
Her mind precise for the journey.
Her soul enflamed for the journey.
Journeyed to the arms of God.

In the warmth of those arms, she knew.
Ancient pathways op'ning before her, she knew.
Words of her people streamed into her heart, she knew.
Knew that her God had come home.

Epilogue
In Gratitude

Miryam, my kinswoman,
I have called your name
        and you have answered me.
Across time and space we have journeyed
        groping through the mist of legend and fantasy
        squinting between the cracks in the dogma-stone
        sensing delicately the palpitations of your life
            beneath blue plaster mantles
            and benign stare-fixed smiles.

Woman of witness.
Woman of prayer.
Woman named the Hebrew name Rebellion.
Share yourself with me, with us,
        this day, this time, forever.